*A COMPILATION OF PRACTICAL STRATEGIES FROM FINANCIAL EXPERTS*

# Building WEALTH

### ENTREPRENEURIAL, PROFESSIONAL, AND FINANCIAL EXPERTISE UNLOCKED

## COMPILED BY AYANNA M. SMITH

**FEATURING:**
EULICA KIMBER • DR. TSCHANNA TAYLOR • KATRINA GARRETT • SAMANTHA BOND

Copyright @ 2024 Ayanna M. Smith
ISBN: 979-8-9860867-6-7
All rights reserved.

Author owns complete rights to this book and may be contracted in regards to distribution. Printed in the United States of America.

**Library of Congress Cataloging-in-Publication Data**

The copyright laws of the United States of America protect this book. No part of this publication may be reproduced or stored in a retrieval system for commercial gain or profit.

No part of this publication may be stored electronically or otherwise transmitted in any form or by any means (electronic, photocopy, recording) without written permission of the author except as provided by USA copyright law.

The Holy Bible, King James Version (KJV) . Amplified (AMP) Copyright © 1954, 1958, 1962, 1964, 1965, 1987 by The Lockman Foundation

Editing: SynergyEd Consulting/ synergyedconsulting.com
Graphics & Cover Design: Greenlight Creations Graphics Designs
glightcreations.com/ glightcreations@gmail.com

Be it advised that all information within this literary work, *Building Wealth*, has been acknowledged to be the truthful accounts of each co-author. The co-authors are responsible for their contributions and chapter accuracy and hold SHERO Publishing harmless for any legal action arising as a result of their participation in this publication.

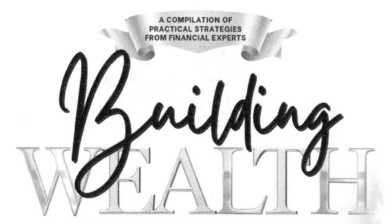

A COMPILATION OF PRACTICAL STRATEGIES FROM FINANCIAL EXPERTS

# Building WEALTH

ENTREPRENEURIAL, PROFESSIONAL, AND FINANCIAL EXPERTISE UNLOCKED

## Table of Contents

**Dedication**   5
**Acknowledgements**   6
**Introduction**   7
  8

### ~Co-Author Chapters~

| | | |
|---|---|---|
| **Ayanna M. Smith** | *Life Insurance is NOT a Curse Word!!* | 10 |
| **Dr. Tschanna Taylor** | *The Sum of Our Journey* | 26 |
| **Eulica Kimber** | *Business By the Numbers: Wealth Through Entrepreneurship* | 42 |
| **Katrina Garrett** | *A Changed Mind* | 62 |
| **Samantha Bond** | *Turning Financial Pain into Profit & Prosperity* | 80 |

# *Dedication*

This book is dedicated to everyone working to build their financial legacy and security. May the resources provide you with the wealth of knowledge needed to help you WIN!

# Acknowledgements

To the Ladies of the ***Building Wealth*** project, with profound gratitude, I extend a heartfelt THANK YOU! Your invaluable contributions to this anthology have left me humbled and inspired. The wealth of knowledge that you've shared, from your respective domains, coupled with the genuine passion each of you brought to this project, has transformed it into a true work of art.

Thank you for not only making this publication a bestseller, but also crafting a guide for women and men alike, fostering a mindset shift in the pursuit, construction, and maintenance of wealth. Each of you has shared a piece of your heart, mind, and expertise, creating a collective masterpiece.

I am totally thankful for the collaborative spirit that permeated our work. Your dedication has not only elevated this book but has the potential to impact and empower countless lives. As we continue this journey, I pray and wish for each of you nothing but continued success and the strength to soar, run your businesses, and reach the masses in multiple arenas.

All the Best!!

*Ayanna*

# Introduction

In the tapestry of life, laughter is the feast, and wine brings merriment, yet it's *money* that echoes through every chapter. Ecclesiastes 10:19 reminds us that every endeavor requires an investment—be it in currency, time, or energy. Nothing we aspire to is achieved on the wings of whims; even the air that we breathe comes at a cost.

As individuals navigating our financial narratives, each of us have embarked on a unique journey. Within the pages of this anthology, we weave together lessons, share personal stories, and offer practical guidance, forging a path toward a resilient wealth-building mindset.

This collection is an invitation for men, women, young adults, and business owners to introspect, relate, and grow—from personal victories to business triumphs. With every turn of the page, envision yourself in the narratives, absorb the wisdom, and fortify your arsenal for wealth creation. ***Building Wealth: Entrepreneurial, Professional, and Financial Expertise Unlocked*** is more than a compilation; it's a key to UNLOCKing mindsets, propelling individuals of all ages towards the realization of not just millions, but boundless possibilities. Let these insights and experiences be your guide on the journey to making millions and more!

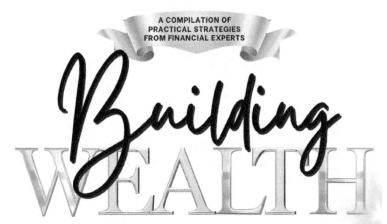

A COMPILATION OF PRACTICAL STRATEGIES FROM FINANCIAL EXPERTS

# Building WEALTH

ENTREPRENEURIAL, PROFESSIONAL, AND FINANCIAL EXPERTISE UNLOCKED

# Chapter 1

*Author Ayanna Smith*

# Author & Visionary
# Ayanna Smith

Hailing from the vibrant city of Hampton Roads, Virginia, Ayanna M. Smith emerges as a beacon of authority and inspiration, especially for professional and entrepreneurial women seeking financial mastery.

With a remarkable background steeped in the world of finance, Ayanna shines as a revered life insurance broker, a prolific four-time published author, motivational speaker, dedicated coach, facilitator and lifelong educator. Her journey reflects a commitment that runs deep, inspired by a lineage of esteemed educators. A graduate of North Carolina Central University with a degree in Elementary Education, Ayanna's expertise flourished, leading her to excel as an accomplished Elementary School Assistant Principal.

Her captivating leadership spans both classroom and administrative domains, resonating effortlessly with scholars and mentors alike. In the realm of finance, Ayanna's passion takes flight as an advocate, empowering individuals and families to navigate their financial landscapes. Her dedication to bridging the gap in historically marginalized communities through conversations about *generational wealth and health* is unwavering, evident in her establishment of a financial literacy office in Portsmouth, Virginia in February 2022.

Ayanna's excitement and thorough knowledge radiates across esteemed platforms where she imparts solid financial counsel, equipping captivated audiences with invaluable tools. Witness her brilliance firsthand on *Money Talks with Ayanna Smith*, her engaging weekly livestream show.

# Life Insurance is NOT a Curse Word!!

**An old, yet important story...**

There was a knock at the door and the ringing of the front doorbell. Ma-Ma asks, "Who is it?" The person at the door says, "It's the insurance man." The door is opened, and the insurance man enters the living room. He enters, sits down and awaits Ma-Ma's return from one of the back rooms. Ma-Ma returns with the money for the payment for the life insurance policy and all is well until the next time the little insurance man returns for the next payment. It's not recalled if he stopped by monthly or quarterly. However, it was an indelible mark made on the mind of the young child watching, observing and wondering what that transaction was all about. Flashing forward approximately 40 years later, that little girl understood what that money paid for and what that life insurance policy meant. Once Ma-Ma passed, life took on a whole new meaning. She was gone, but not without instructions and not without having protected her family from double grief. But, to back track a few years earlier when her husband passed, things were in place and that process also went smoothly due to life insurance preparations. My grandmother didn't have to "figure out" where the money was going to come from. The proceeds had already been prepared and planned out. It gave her time to grieve and not have the burden of being filled with uncertainty and angst.

## PREPARATION REDUCED STRESS

The importance of proper preparation provides a lifted burden from any family. Having some type of insurance plan is an invaluable tool not only in the time of one's passing but can also be an awesome protection while the policyholder is living.

So, let's return to additional pieces of the story. I remember that fretful timeframe of my grandmother's passing. I remember the family: my mother, my uncle, my sister and I gathered together at the funeral home. We had to talk about the laying to rest, the services, and all the breakdown of the funeral costs. Funerals, as most people know, can vary in range of cost from state to state, city to city and town to town. After speaking with a reputable funeral director, I was told that having insurance is not only wise but an absolute necessity. It was also shared that funeral costs have escalated over the years, and it will now take more than $5,000 to handle the final expenses. Therefore, additional insurance may be needed if there's only a $5,000 policy. In other words, "$5,000 is not going to do it" or cover the funeral costs. This means that it's time to reevaluate what's in place and determine if we need more insurance or another type of insurance that's suitable for our current needs. For, there's so much that goes into the planning of the funeral as well as the burial. Some things to consider include the place where the service would be held, and what type of service will be conducted. Will it be in a church, at the funeral home, or graveside; a memorial or a full service? Will there be a selected casket, or will the deceased be cremated? Will there be singers, clergy, flowers, a repast, or even doves released? All those final wishes matter, however, they are all a line item that builds a bottom-line cost. We'd hope to send our loved ones out in the best way possible, but without preparation it could pose an emotional and financial hardship.

Nevertheless, as I reminisce on the time of my grandmother's passing and listening to the funeral director, it was a joy to hear and witness that my grandmother had all her funeral affairs in order; her casket chosen, and money paid up! My grandmother had even shared with me that she wanted to have her 50th wedding tea length dress and veil on when she'd be laid to rest. She left that as a task for me to carry out. And expected me to do so. Of course, I honored her and made sure that the dress and a headpiece/veil were delivered to the funeral home. The only bill that we had to pay was for the service programs. My grandmother and grandfather had their affairs in order; they took full responsibility to ensure that they would exit life with dignity and without burdening their family. Their model has led me to have life insurance and to do the same for my surviving family. None of us know the time or the day we are going to pass, but we will all leave someone on this earth. Based on the model before me, I choose to leave folk with no stress or at least plan not to pose additional stress to an already stressful situation.

With this story in mind, this has led me to see the importance of leaving a legacy. My grandparents left a legacy for me and my family to live on and transition through the grief much better than if we had to come out of pocket or had to get a loan or charge the funeral on a credit card or have to pass the hat and garner funds from relatives, friends, charities and online money requesting links that take part of the money in service fees.

## ONE FAMILY'S DEVASTATION

Although my family didn't have to endure the hardship that some have endured, one or two stories jog my memory; stories of families that were left in disarray when the spouse and children were left without any recourse due to the death of the father.

This story is one of many that could be shared. This couple had life insurance agents visit their home to talk about getting plans in place. The husband scoffed and stated that he had coverage on his job and was okay with that. The agents left without being able to impress on the man of the house to extend his coverage by supplementing what he had on his job. A short time later the man passed in his sleep and the family was devastated. Yes, he had insurance on the job, but it did not cover him outside of his job. His dying at home was not covered. Not only was this total devastation for his family; but, to top it off, the lack of an adequate life insurance policy produced a great financial hardship for the wife. She and her children had to move elsewhere as they were unable to pay the mortgage and remain in their home. The wife was left so grief-stricken that she was unable to work for a stint. She spiraled into a deep depression. The devastation is real and extremely traumatic. However, this does not have to be the ending. Let's focus on rewriting that narrative and view life insurance and other financial matters as a priority.

# STEPS TO CREATING A BETTER FINANCIAL FOUNDATION- BEGINNING WITH LIFE INSURANCE

As we seek a new way or elevated way of thinking about life insurance, here are some things we may not have known or fully realized about the benefits of life insurance. Life insurance serves as a multiple armed strategy for long-term effects on families, individuals and business owners. Glean and implement from the following:

**Financial Security:** Life insurance provides a financial safety net for your loved ones when you pass away. It can replace your income and help maintain their standard of living. Example: If the primary breadwinner of a family were to die, life insurance can cover the lost income, ensuring the surviving spouse and children can continue to meet their financial needs.

**Debt Settlement:** Life insurance can be used to pay off outstanding debts, such as mortgages, student loans, or credit card debt, relieving the burden on your family. Example: If the insured person had a mortgage, the life insurance payout can clear the debt, allowing the family to remain in their home.

**Funeral Expenses:** The immediate costs of a funeral and burial can be significant. Life insurance can ease the financial burden during a difficult time. Example: A life insurance policy can cover funeral costs, ensuring that grieving family members don't have to worry about expenses.

**Education Funding:** Life insurance can help fund education expenses for children or grandchildren. Example: The payout can be earmarked for a child's college education, ensuring their future opportunities.

**Estate Taxes:** Life insurance can be used to cover estate taxes, preserving the value of assets for beneficiaries. Example: Without life insurance, heirs might need to sell valuable assets to cover estate taxes.

**Business Continuation:** For business owners, life insurance can fund a buy-sell agreement, ensuring a smooth transition of ownership upon the death of a partner. Example: In the event of a business partner's death, life insurance can provide the necessary funds for the surviving partner to buy out the deceased partner's share.

**Income Replacement for Stay-at-Home Parents:** Even if a family member doesn't earn a traditional income, their contribution to the household is invaluable. Life insurance can cover the costs of childcare, housekeeping, and other services. Example: If a stay-at-home parent were to pass away, life insurance can cover the cost of hiring help to maintain the household.

**Inheritance Equalization:** Life insurance can help ensure that assets are distributed fairly among heirs.
Example: If one child is inheriting a family business, life insurance can provide a financial equivalent to be distributed to other heirs.

**Charitable Giving:** Some people use life insurance to leave a legacy by naming a charity as a beneficiary. Example: A philanthropist can use a life insurance policy to support a charitable cause they are passionate about.

**Long-Term Care Benefits:** Some life insurance policies offer riders that can provide long-term care benefits, helping to cover the costs of healthcare and support in old age. Example: A policyholder can access their policy's long-term care benefits to cover nursing home expenses, allowing them to maintain their quality of life in their later years.

Although this is not an exhaustive list, these examples illustrate how life insurance can serve as a cornerstone of financial planning, offering peace of mind and financial stability for individuals and their families. It's important to note that the type and amount of life insurance should be tailored to individual circumstances and financial goals.

## QUESTIONS TO ASK YOUR FINANCIAL ADVISOR/ PROFESSIONAL/LIFE INSURANCE BROKER

The information provided in this book is not designed to frighten anyone, rather it's to serve as a guideline for elevated financial prowess. As you're on the financial journey, here are some key questions that may assist in reaching financial goals and help to navigate the life insurance space:

**What Type of Life Insurance is Best for Me?**
Ask the financial professional to explain the different types of life insurance (e.g., term, whole, universal) and help you determine which one aligns with your financial goals.

**How Much Life Insurance Coverage Do I Need?**
Discuss your financial responsibilities and goals, such as debt repayment, income replacement, and education funding, to determine the appropriate coverage amount.

**What Riders or Additional Features Should I Consider?**
Inquire about optional riders, such as critical illness, long-term care, or disability income, and whether they are suitable for your needs.

### What Is the Cost of the Insurance Premiums?
Understand the premium costs for the life insurance policy and how they fit into your budget. Ask about the flexibility of premium payments.

### Is the Policy Portable?
Determine if the life insurance policy can be transferred or continued if you change jobs or circumstances.

### Are There Any Restrictions or Exclusions in the Policy?
Clarify any limitations or exclusions in the policy, such as suicide clauses, contestability periods, or restrictions on high-risk activities.

### How Will This Life Insurance Fit into My Overall Financial Plan?
Discuss how life insurance integrates with your broader financial goals, investments, retirement planning, and estate planning.

### What Happens if I Miss a Premium Payment?
Understand the consequences of missing premium payments and inquire about any grace periods or options for catch-up payments.

### Can I Adjust the Policy in the Future?
Ask about the flexibility to modify the coverage amount, change beneficiaries, or make other adjustments as your circumstances change.

### How Does the Underwriting Process Work?
Learn about the steps involved in underwriting, including medical exams, health assessments, and how your health and lifestyle may affect your premiums. It can vary by company and type of product being sought.

**What Happens in the Event of a Claim?**
Understand the claims process, including who to contact, required documentation, and how beneficiaries will receive the proceeds.

**What Are the Tax Implications of the Policy?**
Discuss the tax treatment of premiums, cash value, and death benefits to ensure your plan aligns with your tax goals. Please seek a tax professional.

**What's the Financial Professional's Compensation Structure?**
Inquire about how the financial professional is compensated, whether through commissions, fees, or a combination of both, to understand potential conflicts of interest.

## CANCELING YOUR POLICY OR MAKING CHANGES

Understand the process for canceling the policy or making modifications and any associated costs or penalties.

Some or all the latter questions will help to make an informed decision when working with a financial professional to create a comprehensive financial plan that includes life insurance. It is imperative to gain a clear understanding of all options and how they align with each unique financial situation and goals.

# CONCLUDING QUESTIONS

Elevating one's financial journey often involves gaining clarity, setting goals, and making informed decisions. Here are three key questions that can help individuals enhance their financial well-being:

### 1. What Are My Financial Goals and Priorities?
Understanding your financial goals is crucial. Ask yourself what you want to achieve in the short-term and long-term. Whether it's buying a home, saving for retirement, paying off debt, or starting a business, clearly defining your objectives is the first step toward success.

### 2. What Is My Current Financial Situation?
To make meaningful progress, you need to have a solid grasp of your current financial standing. This involves asking questions such as:

- What is my income and what are my expenses?
- Am I making enough money?
- Do I need to make more money?
- How much debt do I have, and what are the interest rates?
- How much do I have saved and invested?
- What are my assets and liabilities?

This assessment provides the foundation for creating a budget, managing debt, and building wealth.

### 3. What Strategies Can I Implement to Improve My Financial Situation?
Once you know your goals and understand your current situation, the next step is to determine the strategies and actions needed to reach your financial objectives. This can include creating a budget to manage expenses and save more, reducing high-interest debt, and developing a debt payoff plan. The plan

can also include investing in assets like stocks, bonds, or real estate to grow your wealth.

The prior questions and strategies may vary from situation to situation. It is shared as I speak with potential clients about their financial journey plan, "This is not a one size fits all, but one that fits you." Therefore, having a plan is essential for financial success. The latter questions serve as a framework that will assist in providing definitive goals, assess your current financial situation, and create a roadmap for achieving financial stability and prosperity.

# Chapter 2

*Author*

*Dr. Tschanna Taylowr*

# Author Dr. Tschanna Taylor

Whereas others find their greatest fulfillment and motivation in moving forward, she found hers in looking *back*. Affectionately known as "The Publishing and Marketing Powerhouse," Dr. Tschanna Taylor realized that to effectively build, she had to heal—hurts and wounds that stemmed from as far back as childhood. After exposing those broken places, which spilled over into her spiritual, financial, emotional, and physical life, she made a conscious choice to collaborate with several coaches and therapists—and use those same broken places as building blocks. As an entrepreneur, for over 29 years in business, she's committed to helping others dig through roots in their life and confidently share their message to grow and bear fruits monetizing from their pain.

Dr. Tschanna is a publishing and marketing consultant who teaches female entrepreneurs how to magnetize, monetize, and maximize their message using their book or chapters in book anthologies to feel more at peace and financially secure.

Dr. Tschanna holds several degrees and certifications from DeVry University, Keller Graduate School of Management, and other institutions, focusing on counseling, coaching, and entrepreneurship. Dr. Tschanna Taylor is an international best-selling author, marketplace chaplain, and TEDx speaker. Set apart by her transparent delivery and transformative storytelling abilities, anyone can clearly see that she is resilient about helping others operate authentically and unapologetically in their purpose.

**Connect Dr. Taylor:**
Facebook, Instagram, & Tik Tok @ tschannataylor
Website: www.tschannataylor.com

# The Sum of Our Journey

As a Senior Accounts Receivables Specialist for a state governmental agency, it is my responsibility to record financial transactions of payments received. I perform this task by managing the flow of money between the company and the customers who require state licensing. I post payments in a timely fashion and any outstanding invoices due; I use state-regulated policies and processes to collect said payments.

When the opportunity came to contribute to this anthology, I wanted to draw parallels with the duties I perform in the accounting industry to how these principles relate to us collectively from the basic math lessons we learned as far back as elementary school.

As you continue to read my chapter, I will share a few life experiences I learned, and how they compare to addition, subtraction, multiplication, and division. It is my desire that the information I share relates to you in some way. After reading my chapter, feel free to share with me how these examples have given you an aha moment or made you laugh or look at your situations a little differently.

# BACK DOWN MEMORY LANE

Learning math was fun for me when I was in elementary school. Who knew that the math songs we sang in class with our peers would intrinsically relate to us all, as adults. It was only when I reached the sixth grade at Shepard Middle School that I did not think math was so much fun anymore. However, the math lessons I learned served as the foundation to prepare me for the harder lessons we call **LIFE**. Each grade that I passed, from middle school on, were the steps that taught *the more you elevate, the harder the tests.*

My favorite math teacher at Shepard was Mrs. Icelean Payton. She was an " old-school" teacher. She believed in the thick wood paddles hanging near the chalkboard. Mrs. Payton was the kind of teacher who knew your entire family and did not mind calling them on the phone after 6 p.m. to tell them how you progressed in her class. Lord, have mercy, do not get a math problem wrong because you paid for it by getting your ear twisted and everyone would be laughing as your ear is flaming red while your face is balled up from sheer embarrassment. We do not have teachers like that anymore. Mrs. Payton did not take no mess off any of her students. She was very loving and nurturing but as a 10-year-old, you were not seeing her actions as love. All that was on your mind was waiting for the bell to ring to switch to your next class when it came to her. But what I love most about Mrs. Payton is that she taught us to be flexible and not stay stuck in our comfort zones. She saw our potential when we did not even know what *potential* meant. The lessons she taught me shaped me to be the woman I am today. I love her for the love she gave to me and so many others.

There was only so much she could teach within a six-hour school day. In school, Mrs. Payton taught us math lessons and gave us tests to measure what we learned while in her class. But as adults, The World gives us tests, then teaches us the lesson afterward. Is that not crazy, how as adults we only use a fraction of the math we learned in school! The majority of us do not use algebra, calculus, geometry, or trigonometry, but we all use the basic order of operations in math, right? Then there are the lessons that cannot be taught by our teachers or our parents, but learned the hard way, through making our own mistakes.

The skills that we learned are attributable to our habits. These habits can either hurt us or help us. Did you know that math even has a role to play in the habits we have by making sure we think our decisions through strategically? Learned math skills serve as a framework to guide us to make rational decisions, rather than emotional ones.

Every one of us desires to reach a level of success in our lives. Especially with the many changes we are all experiencing in today's economy. We all have our own definitions of what success looks like, but universally speaking, success is measured by your own definition of what it looks like for you and survival.

The basic math we learned in school serves as the foundation or a universal language for how we handle life tasks. We use basic math from how we measure our exercise by the number of reps or sets we do, how we measure the food to prepare for our annual Thanksgiving family get-togethers, how long it takes for us to drive to see our family for the upcoming holidays to us checking the gas prices comparing it to the gas mileage to get us from point A to point B.

One of the overall principles of a Senior Accounts Receivables Specialist in the accounting industry is to know how to balance on both sides (assets=liabilities + net equity) to find the solution. Whether you realize it or not, you are applying accounting principles in your everyday lives by using the basic math operations of addition, subtraction, multiplication, and division. We live in exceptionally taxing times with a lot of ever-evolving changes. As the world continues to evolve, we must continue to accept and adapt to change even when we do not want to. This is the way Mrs. Payton taught us and to sum it up, life is like accounting- *EVERYTHING* must be in order and *BALANCE*.

## LIFE COMPARED TO MATH: MY LIFE, MY LIFE, MY LIFE!

Allow me to metaphorically share some of my life by attributing these challenges to how basic math played a role in me overcoming or working towards overcoming. Each example I share is distinctive and intertwines numerical actions with real-life experiences that you personally can relate to or may know someone who may have experienced something similar. I plan to give you a unique narrative on how to succeed and continually evolve through life's diverse chapters.

Here are the definitions of the basic math operations so you can get the context of the life challenges I share according to Webster's online dictionary.

**Addition**-*(noun)* the process of adding something to something else.
**Subtraction**- *(noun)* the process of taking one number away from another number.
**Multiplication** – *(noun)* the process of increase in numbers.
**Division** – *(noun)* the process of separating something into parts.

Do you notice that all the definitions have a keyword that repeats itself? It is called PROCESS! Process is the series of steps taken to achieve a particular end. Process is what I had to embrace when going through my struggles. I am the poster child of life challenges, and I will be the first to tell you that the PROCESS DOES NOT FEEL GOOD (in my eye-rolling, "over-it facial expression, as I type this chapter, lol).
Are you ready? Let's go.

# OVERCOMING ILLNESS

Since my early twenties, I was diagnosed with Type II Diabetes. Having this diagnosis has been a hell of a roller coaster ride managing this disease. I did every diet imaginable from Slim Fast and Jenny Craig to the Military Diet. I exercised my tail off and I even tried being a vegan for 2.25 days and as you can see this journey was an **EPIC** fail. I just could not lose the weight. It was only after having to have an emergency gastric bypass surgery from developing gastroparesis (where food wouldn't digest for weeks on end due to poor management of diabetes), being a caregiver to three family members who eventually passed away from diabetes, and questioning who would raise my son like I would if something happened to me, did I decide that I needed to accept and adopt a new mindset.

Old habits were killing me. I experienced so many health challenges from stomach issues to little sexual motivation, to losing 50% use of sight in one eye. All these things happened because of my disobedience to do what was right. I got caught up in my own comfort zone. For example, when the weather got cold, I indulged in eating macaroni and cheese or gumbo with rice and cornbread. Or when at family gatherings, instead of eating more vegetables, I gave myself reasons to have extra servings of mashed potatoes and chocolate cake. Diabetes started out as gestational diabetes and later evolved into full-blown diabetes to now, no longer being classified as a diabetic. And since we are talking about wealth, my diabetes status even affected the medical index when I apply for life insurance; which causes me to pay more in premiums (I understand this because I used to be a life insurance agent. I know, a Jackie-of-all-trades). So, you see, obedience is better than sacrifice. Here is how I applied the basic math operations in this challenge in my life.

***Addition***: I had to add a reset button emotionally, spiritually, financially, mentally, culturally, socially, and more importantly, physically. I had to "count the cost" because the disease was costing me too much in these areas of my life. I had to become more aware of what I was eating and how much I was eating. I had to adopt a positive lifestyle change that meant having more vegetables in the place of carbs, hiring a fitness coach who wouldn't play any games but hold me accountable, and did detoxes every six months to clean all the toxic waste that no longer served me. I ate these vegetables raw for 45 days and let me tell you, I couldn't stand my husband for frying chicken when he knew the battle I was up against. Even when the tests came, I had to kick the tests in the face because I had to overcome or else, I would have had to deal with "something else" and who wanted that? If I ever called on the name of Jesus, whew! I also had to find an exercise plan that worked for me. People mean well and are intentional but there is no *one size fits* *all* way to doing a thing. Try what will work for you. I chose walking, light dancing for the people with two left feet, and cardio-strength training.

***Subtraction***: I had to eliminate the junk food in my pantry and throw away all the foods causing more damage. I had to get rid of stress by putting myself first. I did this by implementing not only self-care but soul-care practices. This required taking inventory of the wounds that went as far back as my childhood; wounds from my mother, father, abandonment, rejection, and trust issues. As part of self-care, I had to change my negative attitude when people who cared would check me on the foods that I was eating.

***Multiplication***: I had to remain positive despite all the negativity I was faced with. I decided to fight with everything within me because I had to remember my greater why, which was to appreciate who God created me to be and be the best mom I could be to my son. I had to increase the vitamins and supplements I was taking to reduce the medications given to me. I had to multiply the number of times I would exercise and do good things for myself.

***Division***: I had to cut out the people in my life who were enabling me to continue to eat wrong and have the wrong mindset towards living a healthier life. I had to remove eating out by learning how to cook my own recipes from my favorite restaurants. I reduced my carb intake and stopped eating bread. I even stopped hanging out at family gatherings for a prolonged period. I figured out how to find balance; I eat before I attend family gatherings and other social events so I do not overeat while still giving them my love and making new memories.

Although we hear medical professionals tell us that the diseases, we are diagnosed with could be hereditary, I can say from my own experiences that not everything I had to overcome, health-wise, was hereditary. I am 100% responsible for my life. Not based on my mother, father, or other family members. Me! I had to accept and adapt to a new lifestyle, and I am happy to share that although this journey has not been an easy one, I am now off of all diabetes medications and down to a size 10 in clothes. This is not to brag in any way. This is to share the journey and how something as simple as math can apply if health is a challenge for you. I am rooting you on because if I can do it, so can you.

## GOODBYE, LOVE (*MARRIED, DIVORCED SELF-EMPOWERMENT*)

There was a song I heard the other day, and the lyrics reminded me of the challenge with being married, separated, divorced, to being self-empowered. I hated to leave but staying was costing me my health, so much so I almost died in 2022. I even cried several times with making a hard decision but, at the end of the day, I had to choose me. It was costing me too much. Health for me as I shared previously was my top priority. There were mother-father wounds, being a bad financial steward, PTSD from experiences in the military, lack of intimacy, and cheating, just to name a few of the reasons that enough was enough. No one ever gets married to intentionally be divorced; sometimes it is okay to bow out gracefully. In no way am I blaming everything on my ex. It took two to get married and it takes two to divorce. The good in this is that we are amicable but wise enough to know that the marriage is beyond reconciliation. My great aunt, Aunt Tee Baby, always used to tell me as a little girl that I never had to accept anyone's *ish* (well she did not say it quite like that, but you get where I'm going, lol). The more we faced obstacles in our marriage and did not communicate well or didn't collectively come with conflict resolution tactics to learn and grow together, the more I discovered we were misaligned and growing apart.

Marriage is easy to get into but hard to get out of. I had to learn how to navigate through the storm of emotions, and financial and social adjustments to lead to my selfempowerment. Allow me to share using the metaphor of basic math operations. The lens of addition, subtraction, multiplication, and division provided me with the structure to move forward to resilience, rebuilding, and redefining Dr. Tee.

***Addition***: Addition did not only represent the need to incorporate a new lifestyle of being a single mompreneur, but it also allowed me to re-add back the neglected parts of myself that I let go to try and hold on to a failed marriage. One of the things that I loved to do before meeting and marrying my ex was playing professional poker. Because my schedule does not allow me to travel to Las Vegas or Atlantic City to play leisurely, I will go hang out at local venues and meet up with some old friends to play for fun. I spent time with my girlfriends, especially the ones who were single discussing ways we can improve in our business, parenting our teenage children, and using the love the Lord left within us to still have room for new love. The same is true; it is no different than investing in your financial portfolio. I became more aware of how I was spending money, time, and investing into my well-being that would give me a successful return physically, financially, and emotionally. Adding was about me embracing new opportunities and positivity in my life that fosters growth and happiness.

***Subtraction***: I had to get used to letting go of the shared responsibilities we had, separating assets, and separating our intertwined lives. There were days the extraction was painful like pruning a plant to allow for new growth. I removed emotional and financial debts that kept me captive. I had to let go of the guilt and regret for leaving; remembering why I left in the first place. I had to remember my value and worth.

***Multiplication***: I took courses and earned certifications that multiplied my self-care techniques; restoring joy during the storms I was facing. I acquired new entrepreneurial skills that allow me to be a publishing and marketing powerhouse today. I traveled a lot for leisure and business; it served to amplify my resilience, joy, and satisfaction. I regularly recited and focused on my favorite scriptures; using them to get me through the tough days and as affirmations to reignite my self-worth, my dreams, and aspirations. Multiplication means abundance, prosperity, and peace. I learned to do the work inwardly so outwardly the two would match up.

***Division***: I was once a married entity now single. Yet it seemed like my responsibilities quadrupled. I had to learn the art of division of my time, energy, and resources so nothing felt like there was any lack or scarcity. I had to distribute my time evenly; spending time with God, myself, my son, working a full-time job, running a business, and working towards my personal development. Strategically, I had to divide resources, investments, finances, and assets to be fair based on the laws in North Carolina. Division showed me how to ensure self-preservation while avoiding emotional exhaustion and nurturing a well-balanced, wholesome existence post-divorce.

**CONCLUSION**

The examples I shared are just snippets of life challenges that I had to learn how to accept and adapt; all while overcoming them. Life is a continuous series of basic math operations. Whether it is managing personal development, financial resources, or relationships; the principles of addition, subtraction, multiplication, and division are interwoven into our daily lives. These simple techniques help us to navigate through the complexities of life. I am reminded of Matthew 14:22 that no matter the problems we are faced with, there is always better on the other side. Life will happen. Recognize change when it happens but be aware of how you respond and remain balanced to get to the solution. This is the sum of our journey.

# EMPOWERMENT MOMENT

Adding, subtracting, multiplying, and dividing are effective tools as we ponder, calculate, and navigate life's journey to shape, refine, and mold our destiny in profound ways. Every new opportunity given to us echoes the promises of ***addition*** for new relationships, new opportunities, and learning new things for our growth. And then there is ***subtraction***, the losses that carve out the things and people that no longer serve us but usher in space for newness coupled with mixed emotions and experiences. ***Multiplication*** amplifies our joys, sorrows, and endeavors to propel us into an expansive world of experiences that mold us to receive increase. Meanwhile, the act of ***division*** beseeches us to balance our time, energy, and resources amidst the myriad challenges, demands, and struggles we face breeding harmony in a chaotic time. For every laugh, tear, and silent compromise, is a basic math operation summing up a beautiful depiction that tells stories of love, loss, pain, and restoration. Let us embark on this journey through the calculations and recalculations we perform every day. May you find echoes of your own basic math operations within my stories and in these mirrored reflections may you discover new insights to decode the sum of your own journey.

**Be empowered!**

# Chapter 3

*Author Eulica Kimber*

# Author Eulica Kimber, CPA

Eulica Kimber has been speaking and teaching the language of business and accounting, for over 30 years. As a Certified Public Accountant (CPA) and Master of Business Administration (MBA), she uses her professional experience in accounting and entrepreneurship to help her clients overcome the fear and intimidation of the numbers of their business by building their business knowledge and leading them to take control of all financial aspects of their operations with confidence. This commitment serves as her inspiration for creating **The Black Woman's Business Bible & Workbook.**

She serves her business coaching clients by creating customized action plans for the startup and growth of companies through her online **Plan2Pro$per Small Business Academy** which also offers her popular self-paced online course, **Accounting Basics for Entrepreneurs**. She is also the author of the **Business by the Number Small Business Planner & Workbook** which is available for purchase on Amazon. All these resources can be found by connecting with Eulica here: https://www.plan2prosperacademy.com/

# Business By the Numbers: Building Wealth Through Entrepreneurship

Entrepreneurship is a powerful means of building wealth. You can start and grow a successful business to accumulate significant assets that can be passed down through generations. I've spent over 30 years helping my clients build and run successful businesses by meeting the needs of their customers or clients. By the way, I will use the terms customer and client interchangeably in this chapter. The term client is most often used to describe patrons of a service-based business and customer is used for a product-based business. But you will notice that I will use both throughout this chapter because the principles can apply to either type of business.

## WHAT IS A BUSINESS?

We will start by defining what a business is. It may seem like common sense, but I've found that in order to master a concept, you must be able to define it. Also, as you will see, there is some confusion around the topic. I define a business as *a recurring revenue-generating activity that provides value that answers a pain point (need or want) of a customer (product) or client (service) with the intent of generating a profit.* I'd like to further examine my definition by discussing key elements of it.

First, a business is a recurring activity. This means if you sell your car once it is not a business. However, if you purchase an inventory of cars with the intent to resale, that is a business and requires you to obtain a business license and take other actions to operate legally. A good business model has the solution to a problem that is recurring. Either customers are repeating patrons like those of a restaurant, or many different people have the same problem. For example, one does not buy a new car every day, but there are many people with that same need, thus supplying a steady pool of buyers.

Second, a business is a revenue-generating activity. This means that you are doing something or selling something in exchange for money. I have met people who believe that they can give away their products or services as a strategy to build clientele. This method rarely works and usually diminishes the perceived value of your offering. What may start as "being a blessing" will likely turn into entitlement. I personally fell prey to this type of thinking in the early days of my accounting firm. As an accountant, I used to give away my services to businesses, churches, and non-profits; believing that I should be a blessing to support their ministry or cause. I found out the hard way that those who didn't pay were the least considerate of my time and demanded increasingly of my knowledge with no intention to compensate me. A 30-minute free consultation would end up costing time away from doing work and from paying clients. Some clients wanted me to walk them through the entire process of setting up their accounting system and to give free advice beyond the free consultation. We will talk about how to price a product or service later in this chapter.

Third, a successful business must offer something that addresses a need or want of the client. There is no such thing as "if you build it, they will come." The most profitable businesses offer something that answers a pain point or strong desire of the customer. I find that some people jump into business without doing their research and end up with a garage full of products that won't sell. Others have invested in a business model that is not in demand. You must become a student of the marketplace. What do people need or want AND are willing or pay for? You cannot build a business in your mind. You must talk to customers and do your homework before jumping into the game.

Now that I have defined what a business is and some elements of a successful business, let's discuss what a business is NOT. A business is NOT a hobby. A business is NOT a nonprofit and a business is not a HUSTLE.

## HOBBY VS BUSINESS

Your business may start from a hobby or passion project, but you cannot jump back and forth between calling it a business or a hobby. IRS Tax Tip 2022-57 dated April 13, 2022, states that a hobby is any activity that a person pursues because they enjoy it and with no intention of making a profit. People operate a business with the intention of making a profit. Many people engage in hobby activities that turn into a source of income. However, deciding if that hobby has grown into a business can be confusing.

To help simplify things, the IRS has established factors taxpayers must consider when determining whether their activity is a business or hobby. These factors are whether:

a. The taxpayer carries out activity in a businesslike manner and maintains complete and accurate books and records.
b. The taxpayer puts time and effort into the activity to show they intend to make it profitable.
c. The taxpayer depends on income from the activity for their livelihood.
d. The taxpayer has personal motives for carrying out the activity such as general enjoyment or relaxation.
e. The taxpayer has enough income from other sources to fund the activity
f. Losses are due to circumstances beyond the taxpayer's control or are normal for the startup phase of their type of business.
g. There is a change to methods of operation to improve profitability.

    h. The taxpayer and their advisor have the knowledge needed to carry out the activity as a successful business.
    i. The taxpayer was successful in making a profit in similar activities in the past.
    j. The activity makes a profit in some years and how much profit it makes.
    k. The taxpayer can expect to make a future profit from the appreciation of the assets used in the activity.

All factors, facts, and circumstances with respect to the activity must be considered. No one factor is more important than another.

If a taxpayer receives income from an activity that is carried on with no intention of making a profit, they must report the income they receive on Schedule 1, Form 1040, line 8.

## NONPROFIT VS BUSINESS

Recently, I've noticed a new trend in questions I've received about people who want to start businesses which are non-profit. I've even seen workshops promoted on social media for this topic. In short, there is no such thing as a non-profit business, and mixing the two concepts will not work out favorably in the long run.

Investopia.com defines a nonprofit organization as *an entity that has been granted tax-exempt status by the Internal Revenue Service (IRS) because it furthers a social cause and provides public benefit.* Donations made to a nonprofit organization are typically tax-deductible to individuals and businesses that make them, and the nonprofit itself pays no tax on the received donations or on any other money earned through fundraising activities. Nonprofit organizations are sometimes called NPOs, or 501(c)(3) organizations based on the section of the tax code that permits them to operate.

If you have a social cause that provides a public benefit, you can start a nonprofit entity; but this means the motive is not to generate profit like it is with a business. You can draw a salary if you provide a service viable to the mission of the organization. However, you also do not have total control of the entity. Usually, nonprofits have a board of directors who share the vision, make decisions, and give directions for the operation of the entity. You cannot OWN a nonprofit. The board has the right and duty to vote you out or fire you if you are not meeting the mission of the organization.

Also, businesses don't accept donations. Your business will receive either revenue from customers, investments from owners, or borrowed money from lenders. This book is about building wealth, and nothing can short-circuit your wealth journey like misunderstanding the rules of the business game. Be clear of the path you want to take and follow the rules of that path.

## A HUSTLE VS A BUSINESS

I define a hustle as an unregistered business. You can only get but so far by operating "under the table" or "bootleg." To be effective and prosperous, a business must be organized and compliant. It is important that your customers, vendors, lenders, and even the government see your business as a professional organization. You should know what you sell, who you sell it to, and be able to operate legally. This means your business is registered with federal, state, and local authorities and your brand is also registered and protected. If you're doing business under a name different than your own, you'll need to register with the federal, state, and local governments depending on your state.

You need to do your homework to determine the requirements for where you live and operate your business. You will need an employer identification number (EIN) from the IRS to open a business bank account and pay taxes. And some states require you to get a tax ID as well. You will also need licenses and permits which vary by industry, state, location, and other factors. Staying legally compliant will ensure that you are able to obtain funding and ensure your account for all expenses, including taxes and fees, when pricing your products and services.

# TRANSLATING YOUR CURRENT SKILLS INTO BUSINESS INCOME

For many years, my mom worked full-time in the house-keeping department at a local hospital in my hometown. In her off hours she also cleaned the houses of the doctors and nurses as a side business. She was also well-known in our community as a cook and baker. Our home was always filled with cakes, pies, and meals for people who paid her to cook for family, church, and community events. My dad owned a lawn business and owned a dump truck. My parents both worked full-time jobs while working their side hustles. My brother and I used to work in their businesses and our family lived a good life.

Why am I sharing this story with you? I want you to know that you can start a business today. You are equipped to generate business today! People are always looking for glamour in business. They want an Instagram-worthy business where they post reels and think that the money will just roll in. While I don't have a problem with this model, please don't miss the money that is right at your fingertips. I challenge you to start with the path that uses your current skills and abilities to start building your empire. You do not have to do this business forever, but it will give you financial seed money while allowing you to enjoy some of the profits to make your life better.

I'd like you to look around you and think about what you have access to that can create income for you this week! If you already have a business, what additional lines of income could you generate by adding a feature, service, or product that you already have experience with?

To illustrate how this works, let's imagine you are a makeup artist. You are very skilled in doing your makeup and makeup for others. You may have past work experience working with one or more makeup brands in a major department store. You have a working knowledge of makeup and skin care products, brushes, and techniques for application. After leaving the makeup job, you occasionally do makeup for friends or family. You want to start a business related to makeup and you must decide what you can offer to customers. We will use this case study to learn about product and service options, how to package, prices your offerings, and key metrics you need to know to be profitable.

## PRODUCTS AND SERVICES

Now that you've decided that you want to use your experience with makeup to start a business, you need to decide how you will meet the needs of your customers. Your business model may be to supply products, services, or a combination of products and services. With our makeup artist example, you may decide to do the makeup for a few weddings and events. The problem with a service business is that it takes YOU to be present every time the service is delivered. This could be very demanding of your time and may require travel to the event locations. These factors must be considered in managing your business costs.

Another business option could be to sell product to another company as an independent contractor. A product is *a tangible or uniquely identifiable item that can be sold and delivered in a single sale.* It can be physical or electronic and may be shipped or maybe a digital asset. It may also be the ticket to an event. The key here is that it can be sold as a single item. Physical products require the purchase of inventory and shipping, and these extra costs should be factored into the sales price or passed along to the customer as an added cost (i.e. shipping cost). You must also manage returns and refunds. Finally, business income is earned upon delivery of the goods.

A service on the other hand has one main feature: YOU! Service-based businesses require you and/or one or more employees to deliver the performance of a task or job or to provide an experience that meets the needs of a client. Pricing your services depends on the type of service, the skill level of the person(s) delivering it, and the demand for the service. Business income is earned when the agreed-upon service is completed or incrementally at major milestones outlined in a contract.

**PREPARING AND PACKAGING YOUR OFFERING**

Now that you have decided what product and or service you can provide to a customer in exchange for money, you must figure out how you will organize and deliver the product or service to the marketplace and collect payment. For example, let's continue with you as a makeup artist. There are several things you can do with this skill set. You can do makeup for weddings or other events. Or you can host workshops teaching clients how to apply their own makeup and skincare basics. Or you can create your own makeup line or do a combination of all these activities. The wonderful thing about entrepreneurship is that you get to explore the best path that brings profit.

Of the choices noted above, the lowest entry cost and easiest profit for this example would be hosting a virtual workshop and allowing people to use their own products. If we decided to start with the workshop, we would look for a platform to host the workshop and a way for people to register and pay. For example, we may use a site like Eventbrite to sell tickets and supply a Zoom link to the customer upon purchase. Next, you will promote the workshop on social media. You may add a product component to the sale by mailing a makeup brush set to registrants.

## PRICING YOUR OFFERING FOR PROFIT

Everything you have at the job should be in place for your business (health insurance, life insurance, taxes, retirement funds). The revenue of your business should cover these costs; so, thought must go into growing your business while making sure that your personal needs are taken care of. This may mean you have to have multiple sources of income to sustain yourself. You may need to maintain employment with another company that provides benefits and income while running your business. This will allow you to build a product and income mix that is proven and enduring to later replace your employment before taking the leap. Or you may even decide to keep employment with another company while running your business. The choice is yours.

Rule number one for pricing is "no pulling prices out of thin air!" Pricing is a formula that includes all the costs for producing or creating the product or service and adding a profit margin. The cost includes those for materials, labor, shipping, taxes, and other fees. So, all expenses of your business should be covered by the sale of your products or services. This includes income tax! I am always confused when business owners are so stressed by income taxes. Income tax, like any other expense, must be estimated and allocated (or distributed) to every sale you make. For example, last year your total income tax for the business was $5,000 or $417 per month. Say, you serve 20 clients a month. That means your price to the client should include about $21 to cover your income tax. You will repeat this calculation for every business expense like rent, subscriptions, and travel costs. Some costs you will be able to link directly to a specific product or service; for example, shipping cost or credit card processing fees. However, some costs are overhead costs, meaning they are the general cost of running your business. Overhead costs will have to be allocated with the estimated dollar amount to add to each sale. Keep in mind that the customer will not see these costs. They will only see the total price that you charge them. I know that this is a lot of work. But what is worse, would you rather get to the end of the year and find that you didn't make enough to cover your expenses and generate a profit?

# MANAGING YOUR BUSINESS BY THE NUMBERS

Yep! Business owners do homework! You must get comfortable with the business numbers to make sound decisions so your business can grow and prosper. Profit is generated from one sale at a time, and you must manage your "business by the numbers" to ensure success.

To run your business by the numbers, you must get comfortable with the financial outcomes of your business. This planner includes monthly, quarterly, and annual worksheets for tracking your key metrics. Business metrics are quantifiable measures used to track business activities to determine the performance level of your business.

**Revenue/Income**: "Money In" or all money earned and/or collected while conducting business

**Expense**: "Money Out" or all money spent to operate your business that is not tied directly to the production and sale of a product

**Cost of Goods Sold (COGS)**: All the money paid out as a cost directly related to the sale of products.

**Gross Profit**: Also called gross income. It is calculated by subtracting the cost of goods sold from revenue. Gross profit only includes variable costs and does not account for fixed costs (overhead). Gross profit assesses a company's efficiency in using its labor and supplies to produce goods or services. It is calculated by starting with Total Revenue and subtracting the Cost of Goods Sold

**Net Income/Net Loss:** "The bottom line." It is calculated by starting with Total Sales Income and subtracting total expenses for a period within a business entity.

## BUILDING WEALTH BUSINESS TIPS:

### Call-To-Action Questions for Business Success

- ☐ What is the customer's need that you want to address?
- ☐ What skills, abilities, and resources do you need to create a product or service to meet the customer's pain point?
- ☐ What is your product or service?
- ☐ How will you deliver it to the customer?
- ☐ What costs need to be considered in the pricing of your product or service?

# Chapter 4

*Author Katrina Garrett*

# Author Katrina Garrett

Katrina Garrett, a native of Norfolk, Virginia, has been married to Tabin G. Garrett since 2010. She has over 20 years of experience in the healthcare industry, implementing and supporting financial systems. She has been sought after to present at various technical conferences over the years. In addition to her profession in the marketplace, she also serves in the ministry. In 2018, Katrina launched, *I Am New LLC (IAN)*, a ministry devoted to the liberation of all people, including those who are burdened, broken, and bound financially, emotionally, and/or spiritually.

While working under *IAN*, she realized that she also had a passion for helping others build and foster healthy relationships. This led her to become a certified Life Coach through the Intercontinental Coaching Institute. Now, Katrina and her husband are Coach Trainers and own, *A New Mind Coaching Academy*. Together they share in the purpose of "Empowering people to be healthy, whole, and achieve their dreams."

Recently she has launched two new initiatives. She established the *Working Woman,* a community to connect and encourage all working women. And finally, she has established *The Renewed Mind Group,* to teach others how to walk in freedom in their minds.

Katrina is a multi-faceted woman who does all things in love and a spirit of excellence. She is known as a Kingdom Encourager, and she desires for everyone she meets to understand that they are seen, have value, and were created on purpose with purpose.

**For more information about Katrina and the services she offers, please access her website: https://katrinagarrett.com/**

# A Changed Mind

My first exposure to money was playing the game of Monopoly. No matter which game piece you chose, everyone started off with the same amount of money. You just rolled the dice, and the strategy was already in place to secure property; whether you landed on streets or railroads. Then the sure $200 just for passing "Go" made it seem that building wealth was a simple task. It was easy money, with the greatest hustle being to roll the dice well. If only life could be like Monopoly.

As I grew up, I saw my family spend their last on Christmas gifts. This way of thinking influenced me to look to money as a means of getting stuff. Fast forward, I went to college to get that "good" degree to make that "good" money. I had no idea that the student loan police would be in hot pursuit of me after graduation. No one told me water and heat bills in older homes are quite expensive. My *"roll of the dice"*, in reality, didn't look like the Monopoly game. I did not start off with the same money as everyone else; Uncle Sam did not grant me the $200 or guaranteed money upon crossing over into each new year. I could barely afford rent; so, the idea of owning a home was simply a fairy tale. My credit card debt continued to soar as student loan payments kicked in. If you put my debt and income on the balancing scale, let's just say the scales did not tilt in favor of my income; my income had little or no weight.

As time went on, I looked forward to those very rare occasions when I made it to payday with my account in the black. If truth be told, I should have owned stock in Bank of America for all the overdraft fees that I incurred. Here, I was thinking that red marks on paper were limited to the classroom, only to discover that I would see a different kind of red on my bank statements. If my bank statements were submitted as a grade for my adult life, it would be safe to say that I was failing miserably. And what was my solution to resolve my red balance issue? It was to get a second job, in addition to my main job, so I could make more money. I ran the figures, did the math and the calculation showed that a $5k increase in my annual salary would help me cover all my bills. Well, guess what happened next? I made $5k more, $10k more, $17k more, and I was still broke. I had more money, but I was still in the red, working to pay down my ever-increasing debt and I still didn't own a home.

So, then the moment happened; I landed the ideal job! However, it required me to travel. Unfortunately, my credit was so bad that I could not qualify for a company card; I would have to pay for my travel out of pocket. That would not have been too bad, except for the fact that my personal credit card was maxed, and the credit card company was not open to extending my credit line. Now to travel, one must understand that you need a major credit card to secure your hotel and car rental. I was left with only one option, which was to pay my credit card down enough so that I could travel each week. I was making decent money, but now some of my money was tied up in travel expenses. At my wits end, I did something that I had never done before, I prayed to GOD to teach me how to better manage my money. I was educated; I had finally reached the place where I made good money. However, the math wasn't matching up in my bank account. I had the increase, but I wasn't *seeing* the increase.

It was after that prayer that GOD began to teach me the importance of stewardship. He took me on a journey of changing my mind on how I viewed and managed money. It was on this journey that I learned that although I prayed for more, I was not in a position to receive the more for which I had prayed. I wanted to see the answer to my prayers reflected in my bank account balance; whereas GOD was teaching me to expand my capacity so that I may be able to receive the more. I had changed jobs but had never changed my mind concerning how I managed my money. This is where I learned the principle that GOD will never give you more than HE can trust you to steward. I was seeking more money, but HE needed me to increase my capacity to manage the more. As we took the journey to a healthier financial me, I saw the increase as HE transformed my mindset about money.

I was never taught how to effectively manage money, but I definitely knew how to spend it. If you have a desire to have more money but your bank account looks like mine did, then GOD is saying to you "If you change your mind, you will ultimately change your money". Now if you are anything like me, you may have tried to bargain with GOD by saying, "If you let me get this much more money, then I will start doing XYZ." GOD's rebuttal to me was, "If you are faithful over the little things then I will make you ruler over much." The principles that I will share with you don't just apply to personal finance, but also your business finances. While I am still writing my story concerning my finances, I will say that in this chapter of my life, I now make over seven times my starting income that I made after graduating college.

Are you ready to build your own generational wealth and be made ruler of much? If this is you, then these are the steps to take to change your mind concerning money.

## BROKE THOUGHTS

*Broke thoughts* translate to *broke talk*, which ultimately leads to a *broke walk*. Broke thinking is the root of almost all money issues. The challenge for me and many of us, is that we are unable to identify that we have *broke thoughts* concerning money. This is because we have normalized *broke thinking* because it is rooted in our belief system.

To use myself as an example, I purchased a brand-new truck with a $400 monthly payment. About two years into having my truck, I took it in to get serviced and the salesperson talked me into purchasing a USED car that had a sticker price of $12k. This used car was a luxury car with leather seats and a sunroof. My new car payment was going to be $525 a month. I was told that was a good deal, I mean it was only $125 more than my other car payment. It wasn't until after I paid off the car that I reviewed the contract and realized that I paid 60k for this used car once they tacked on the balance of my truck plus interest. Let me say that again, I paid $60k for a USED car which is more than I would have paid had I not traded in my new truck. There was absolutely nothing wrong with my NEW truck, but I traded it in for a used car. I was more concerned with proving to others that I looked successful without realizing that my decisions were making me a slave to debt.

I had *broke thoughts* of how I viewed money. Remember, at a young age, I learned how to spend money, but I never understood the principle of saving and investing it. Yes, I saved but only with the thought in mind of how I would spend it. I mean who needs life insurance, right? If I could use a quote from an old commercial to describe my view about money, it would be this, "it is my money and I want *It* now"!

How do you think about money? Do you spend more than you save? If that is the case, you must ask yourself, "What in my thinking makes me feel that I have to spend all my money?" Now I am not suggesting that you don't spend money on yourself, but what I am suggesting is that you spend it within reason. Think over your life's experiences from childhood to now. Are your spending habits learned behavior? Are you an emotional spender? By that I mean, do you purchase items to feel better? We often talk about emotional eating but there is also such a thing as emotional spending. Do you spend money to compensate for a void in your life? Did you grow up in poverty and make a vow to yourself to never be in that situation again? Do you overspend to compensate for a childhood trauma? If any of these questions ring true to you, then you have *broke thinking* concerning money. The thing about broke thinking is that it creates a crack in your financial security. No matter how much you make, it will always seem as though you have holes in your pockets because you have money, but you can never attest to where it goes.

*It is out of the abundance of the heart the mouth speaks.* Matthew 12: 34 When we think broke, we will talk broke. When you talk about money, what do you release over your life? Are you saying things like, "I am always going to struggle", "I can't catch a break", or "This must be my life". Please know that your confession is your declaration. You shall have what you decree. So, I challenge you to have a new declaration concerning your financial situation. They say that insanity is doing the same thing over and over and expecting a different result. In order to have a new confession about your financial situation, you must first develop a new way of thinking concerning how you view money.

# A TRANSFORMED MIND

The word "stewardship" means *to govern over money based on your capacity*. The Bible teaches us that it is important that stewards be found trustworthy. When reading the story of the Parable of the Talents (Matthew 25), it states that GOD gave each servant talents according to their ability. Monopoly had me thinking we should all start with the same finances, but GOD showed me that HE does not release more than HE is able to trust us to steward. In order to be a better steward over your finances you must first be able to replace old thinking with new thinking.

Let's first discuss the principle of needs versus wants. Needs are the things you CANNOT live without, whereas, wants are desires but not necessities. An example of a need is water; we need water to survive. A want would be the desire for flavored water. Flavored water is a preference, not a necessity. GOD promises to supply all of our needs. The challenge is we are often guilty of prioritizing our wants over our needs. Think of those times when you saw a nice pair of shoes and said to yourself, "I need those shoes in my life." In that moment, you have unconsciously classified a want as a need and in some cases, you may forego paying for a valid need (i.e. a utility bill) in order to satisfy your want. If you are going to increase your capacity to be positioned for greater wealth, then you must first be able to prioritize your needs over your wants. Going back to the used car scenario. I did not need to purchase another vehicle, I WANTED to purchase it. My bank account was already swimming in the red, but I wanted that car so badly that I convinced myself that I needed it, which only led to further debt.

Secondly, a good steward must be disciplined in the management of their finances. Pope Francis said it best, "Money must serve, not rule". Are you chasing the money or is the money chasing you? If you are chasing money, then you are not applying self-control. Instead, you are being controlled by money. Self-control can be challenging when we live in an era of instant gratification; a time when we want everything right now. Self-control is about being able to apply the "wait" to the process of building wealth. To put it differently, a seed planted does not produce overnight. First, it sprouts roots underground before you see the branches and later the fruit. The deeper the roots, the more sustainable the tree. However, for a seed to take root, it must first be planted. When building wealth, you must understand that sustainable wealth does not spring up in a short period of time. When you talk about investments, ventures, 401k plans, and life insurance, you have to be both submitted and committed to the process of "waiting". The best way that I can describe the process is that you must be willing to do what you have to do now, in order to do what you WANT to do later. If you always yield to instant gratification, then you will always circumvent the process of building wealth that occurs during the wait.

The challenge that many face is that we eat and or wear the seed instead of planting/sowing it. Starting out, I was guilty of having a plan for my paycheck, and every time there was a raise, I just found something else to purchase. When you receive an increase in money, what thoughts go through your mind? Do you plan to spend, save, or invest? You may be reading this while saying to yourself, "I don't make enough money to do all those things." If so, then what is the first thing you think to do with extra money? As for me, my goal was to always spend first. GOD began to teach me in this area. HE reminded me, that HE gives seed to the sower and began to teach me the principle of sowing and reaping. As I applied the principles learned, I began to put GOD first in my finances and this led to me becoming more disciplined in my spending because I wanted to be obedient to what HE was telling me to do. It was like GOD was my certified financial coach and I was seeing the fruit of this transformation. I slowly began paying off my debts. I was no longer living from paycheck to paycheck. I had eventually graduated to not even recalling my paydays. I filtered my purchases through this one question, "Katrina, is this a need or want?"

As part of my self-discipline, I had to also learn to tell myself, "No". Your "No" does not just apply to yourself but should also apply to others. I have learned that sometimes it is easier to tell yourself "No" instead of others. However, please understand that a withheld "*No*" can sometimes hinder GOD's process of increasing your capacity for more wealth. Now, at this point you may be saying, "No one can hinder what GOD has for my life. What's for me is for me!" And while that is true as pertains to other people; however, it is our inability to say "*No*" that can hinder us.

I had a friend who needed money for something. I loved my friend and supplied the money. Later, this friend was in a bind and asked for money again. I didn't want to say "No" because I had the money to give but I heard GOD say to me, "If you provide the money, you are strengthening the hands of the enemy." My friend was going through a difficult situation that GOD was working on. GOD showed me that by giving the money I was hindering what HE was trying to do. There is a fine line between *enabling* and *helping*. To *help* is to empower someone to do better. *Enabling* does not help a person get out of a difficult situation, but instead keeps them in a place of perpetual bondage. As you learn self-discipline, it is important to understand the power of your "No." Do not allow your "Yes", due to fear of offense, to put you in financial bondage. We must be in tune with our spending even as it pertains to what we spend on others. There are times when a "No" is required. If we don't heed the "No" then GOD will tie our hands.

## FROM THOUGHTS TO ACTIONS

At this point, hopefully, my examples have caused you to reflect on your personal spending habits. In this section, we will discuss practical ways to manage your money. In corporate America, you will not find a successful business that has not set up its budget for the year. A budget is the spending plan for your finances. Whether personal or business, a budget helps you set obtainable goals for your finances. My motto is "if you fail to plan then you are planning to fail." A good budget clearly defines visible and measurable targets for you to achieve. Two reasons why people do not create a budget are that it takes a lot of time, or they do not know how to create a successful budget. Despite these reasons, the end product is well worth the effort.

Things to consider when you set out to write a budget are to write down all expenses and categorize needs versus wants. Also, write down your income. As you write your budget, be sure to budget your savings because life will happen. Savings are an important part of the budget because they account for the unknown. I have seen many people choose not to save anything because the amount they had to save didn't seem like that much. Do not fall into the trap of not saving anything; something is always better than nothing. If possible, do not budget your conditional income such as overtime pay or child support. The reason why is because if your budget is based on your income plus all your conditional income, then you may not be able to sustain that income amount if something happens to your conditional income. For example, let's say you make $3k a month with your base pay and you bring in an extra $1k a month with overtime pay; however, you only work overtime four months out of the year. If you were to purchase a home with a mortgage based on your income with overtime, you would be in a deficit for the majority of the year.

If you plan to make a new purchase (ex. a new car or home), get an idea of what your monthly payment will be and save the difference without spending it monthly. An example would be you pay rent for $1900 a month, and if you buy a home, your estimated mortgage will be $2200 a month which is $300 more a month. This means that you should be able to save $300 ABOVE your regular savings. In other words, if your savings aren't growing by an additional $300+ per month, then $2200 would be too much for you.

If your debt is greater than your income, then look for ways to reduce your expenses. Expense reduction tips include reducing the number of times you eat out, cutting cable options, and focusing on paying down small debts first. If your expenses are extremely higher than your income, consider additional job options or downsizing. Sometimes you must take a step back to propel forward. If downsizing is an option, don't view it as a setback but instead see it as a setup for something greater. Call creditors and arrange to spread out your payment across pay periods. Always try to pay your bills during each pay period. This ensures you pay your bills first and protects you from accidentally spending bill money because it was sitting in your account. If you get paid bi-weekly, you will eventually get ahead of your payments.

Remember that the key to accessing generational wealth is capacity. Your capacity will be tested in how you steward the little you have. The "more" is released to the disciplined, those who are both obedient and trustworthy. I believe we all have the power to attain wealth; however, that does not necessarily translate to sustaining wealth. A builder of generational wealth prepares for long-term gain over instant gratification. They live in the present with the future in mind. The question I leave you with is, "Are you ready to commit to the process of building generational wealth?"

## Wealth Questions:

- What are your financial goals?
- Do you know the amounts in your bank accounts?
- Can you write down ALL your expenses and categorize them as needs versus wants?
- Do your spending habits align with your financial goals?
- What areas can you cut back on in your spending?
- Are you committed to saving and investing for your future?

# Chapter 5

## Author Samantha Bond

# Author Samantha Bond

Samantha K. Bond is a Mogul, Multi business entrepreneur, publisher, author, and highly sought-after business credit instructor coach and woman who at 26-years-old quit her 9-to-5 job and tried her hand at entrepreneurship. Using the skills that she developed in college and Corporate America, sound judgment and sage intuition, she mastered the art of building business credit and accessed over $2 Million in business credit in her first year in business. Samantha became a huge success as she created products to share strategies including her master class that became famous success following that, Samantha received countless television and media features with well-known media outlets??

Today, Samantha is living the life she loves and enjoys using her extraordinary gifts, she has developed a significant following among entrepreneurs around the world, who seek her wisdom, advice, and coaching. Teaching from the heart and armed with a tremendous amount of life and business lessons, she has a knack for touching lives and helping people grow their businesses. As a Coach/Instructor, Samantha shares her story of faith, sacrifice, and determination in the most real and charismatic way while inspiring audiences across the globe. Samantha is a true entrepreneur in every sense of the word.

Samantha's Master Class "How to Access the Millions with Business Credit" by starting a Business provides step-by-step instructions empowering and encouraging people around the world to build their businesses, communities and families through entrepreneurship. Her recently launched Master Class which features step-by-step instruction on how to start a business, and build business credit. Her books can be found on Amazon.com.

Samantha's college education in business, marketing, experience with government agencies include DC Council, years of philanthropic initiatives, real estate investments, business and leadership.

Samantha K Bond's most requested training topics include: Business Credit & Entrepreneurship. She puts constituents together with organizations. With those ingredients, this is where "the magic" happens and there's huge potential for significant economic success.

Samantha's goal is to bless as many moms, entrepreneurs, organizations, and decision makers, improve their bottom line, assist in building and leverage of resources, and find creative ways to help them all expand.

Moms, Entrepreneurs, Organizations & companies like yourself have trusted Samantha to assist them through the business administration & support… to reach short-term and long-term business goals. Samantha has assisted Executives, Council Members & Ambitious Entrepreneurs become more active by contributing tremendous amounts of energy and productivity and step by step strategies.

# Turning Financial Pain into Profit and Prosperity

———— • ————

*I pray that this is a story that helps to turn your financial pain into profit and prosperity. May this be a strategy to add to your arsenal in breaking generational curses. Throughout my chapter, I will be offering financial lessons and the strategies to overcome money problems so that you will stop existing and start living the life of your dreams.* Samantha Bond

I thought I was living the life of my dreams. I had a prosperous career in one of the hottest and sexiest industries in the world. I was making a great living as an executive assistant, and I had a $1 million view of the DC skyline from my waterfront apartment. I drove a luxury convertible Audi and a Mercedes-Benz SUV. I would only dine at five-star restaurants, always; and I was consistently committed to spa appointments.

I always switched up my hairstyles, and I wore the latest designer fashion trends. Although I thought that I was living the dream of a successful black woman in America, I was not content with life. In fact, I suffered from depression, because, in reality, I was *broke*!

But I didn't start that way…

I had humble beginnings, and though I was born with a burning desire to succeed, I was yet to find the vehicle to take me to the heights I was destined to reach.

At the beginning of my journey, I was an unemployed single mom with no family or friends nearby. Success didn't seem to be anywhere close. For a while, I was suicidal, depressed, facing a life-threatening illness, and completely broke!

But even during all those times in my life, I still had a dream. Deep down, I knew I could rise above it all. I was determined never to be a product of my environment. I decided to succeed!

Finally, I was employed; I was working in a collections department earning $13 an hour. I managed to collect over $1 million in closed accounts, and my accomplishments secured me a raise. However, the day I realized my raise was a mere 25 cents an hour was the day that changed my life.

I found my calling in Business Credit. One year later, I managed to access over $2 million in business credit in one day. It changed my life.

My resilience, strength, and fight led to my success, and it's proof of just how quickly anybody can win— no matter what their circumstances are.

The most difficult thing for me was to explain to my loved ones how unhappy I was. I had accumulated a substantial amount of debt, and I was unable to attend any trips with friends or family because I could not afford the charge on my credit card or pay with cash. I felt as if I was drowning, and I was looking for a better life. I had previously experienced anxiety attacks, and fluctuations in weight because of the feeling of defeat; the feeling of being broke.

Can you relate?

There was one incident when I went to the hospital in Washington, DC. I had experienced an anxiety attack and almost fainted from severe chest pains and struggled to breathe as I gasped for air! The doctors tested me and explained that there was nothing wrong with me and that I just needed to stop worrying. I finally saw that if I was ever going to be truly successful, not just financially, but emotionally, and spiritually, I was going to have to do things God's way. My broke mindset caused me to be more concerned with being the boss and earning six figures than being in alignment with God.

Working in a political arena has taught me to capture processes in a systematic fashion. During my mindset transformation, consistency in prayer was a major key in developing and aligning my relationship with God. After surrendering to God, and having my calling revealed, it was time for me to help women and men become economically free.

I put my "business executive" brain to work, sat down at my laptop, and started creating the tools and products to deliver strategies with assistance from God. Then I developed my *millionaire vision plan!*

When developing this business plan, my coaches recommended conducting an analysis of myself and the business. To be honest, there are a lot of people who fail to plan. This results in a cost called failure. If you're waking up, excited to serve God and willing to be used by God as a blessing to others, there lies the true definition of abundance.

I am providing you with the strategies to serve as a diagram for what guided me out of brokenness. I went from being technically broke to now being a woman of abundance. In a matter of less than two years, I can now say that I was able to access over $1 million in business credit, and now I am working towards my ministry and executing my calling by coaching women and men nationally and internationally. My next goal as an advisory coach is to be a career consultant to major and developing organizations.

Decide to walk away from the broke mindset and take the road less traveled to reach your destination of abundance. Let's review my journey; I realized I was living the dream life in a glamorous industry with a million-dollar view in Washington, DC. I drove luxury cars, dined at top restaurants, and stayed committed to spa appointments.

Yet, despite appearing successful, I was unhappy due to debt and health issues. An anxiety attack sent me to the hospital. I realized I needed a change, shifted my focus to align with God, and started helping others financially.

To begin my transformation, I developed a plan with coaches, emphasizing the importance of planning and serving God. Went from broke to abundant life in under two years, with strategies including accessing $1-2 million in business credit.

Now I'm developing products, offering masterclasses and coaching internationally, and aiming for a career consultant role! Will you choose the path to abundance over a broken mindset?

> *You can borrow $1 Million Dollars faster than you can ever earn it as an employee. It may take you twenty years to earn it, but you can borrow $1 Million in six months, if you just have the blueprint to do so.*
> *Financial Freedom will never come where ignorance exists.*
> **Samantha Bond**

I want to share this secret strategy with you that changed my life. By age 26 I discovered how to access millions of dollars in credit funding by implementing business credit strategies that still work!!

You must be wondering, what the heck this woman is talking about, or has she gone crazy?

You might ask: *But, Samantha, how can I do this when I am clueless and fearful about my business finances?*

Right now, you have the choice to focus fully on the infinite possibilities in front of you. **With Smart Strategies you will never run short of business funding and access to business credit!** No matter what your credit score is, 0-850!!! Let's face it, you could waste endless hours and energy trying to figure out where to focus your precious time, what vendors, cash credit cards, and banks to apply to, and what to do next on your own. So, it is best to learn from the masters and SAVE the MONEY, TIME, and ENERGY you would waste trying to do things on your own. Because it is a fact that you can't do everything on your own. To get the most out of anything, you need the expertise of people who have been crushing it for years.

I am here to walk you through step-by-step to help you shave hours... days... weeks, months, and even years... off your learning curve. I've designed my **Value-bomb Masterclass** specifically for people who want to build tremendous amounts of business credit without putting their personal credit at risk and have made the process:

★ Simple to follow
★ Easy to apply
★ Proven to work
★ Affordable for everyone!

I'm not a self-proclaimed guru and I'm not selling you eBooks or videos. I'm an entrepreneur who owned several businesses and stumbled across something called business credit. That was many years ago, and the rest is history, as they say. Take a few minutes to read this; you'll learn how YOU can use business credit to transform your financial situation, regardless of your personal credit, years in business, background, education, or income level. I'm living proof.

I want to share this secret with you that changed my life. I know it will change your life and empower you forever. I want to show you what my millionaire mentors showed me that I am currently implementing in my life now!! I had bad credit. My credit score was 540, which is considered poor. Can you relate? My mentors showed me how to access thousands, even millions, literally in less than two weeks without using my personal consumer credit. In addition, this powerful secret helped me improve my personal credit score which is now above 799-809 and rising.

I understand where you are. I've been there. We are in this together and I'm here to help you. We are going places, you and me. I have traveled the journey that you are on today. I have already reached a destination, and I am here to shorten your learning curve on your path to success. I've done it and I've helped others do it, and here is proof.

*By this means (fractional reserve banking) government may secretly and unobserved, confiscate the wealth of the people, and not one man in a million will detect the theft.*
**John Maynard Keynes**

I will show you what I implemented step-by-step; I will show you how to get credit and cash approvals for your business!

**Did You Know:**

- You can open a business
- You don't need a PG-Personal Guarantee (PG is using your personal credit as a guarantee)
- You don't need your social security #
- You don't need a credit score
- You don't need a Paydex score
- And you don't need a credit history

**Question #1:** Did you know that all you have to do is file a document in your state that will create a business the same day? (INC, LLC, etc) (Monday- Friday. In some states you can register on Saturdays)

**Question #2:** Did you know that you can register your business entity in your state individually, online, or with an attorney?

**Question #3:** Did you know that you can "File for the EIN" the same day, too? And it's free. Go online to IRS.gov, register, and complete the SS4 form after you have registered your business.

It's that easy! So simple right?

*Though the process impoverishes many,*
*it actually enriches some.*
**John Maynard Keynes**

The steps that I will share with you are the exact same steps that I used to access tremendous amounts of business credit and up to $2 million in business funding.

**IMPORTANT FREE TIPS FOR YOU TO GET STARTED:**

**Step #1.** File your business with your local Secretary of State. (Request Form: Articles of Incorporation, then choose your desired formation: CO, INC, LLC, Nonprofit, etc.) There is a small fee for registration in each state. Note: You can walk into your local office, file online, or call your local office of business registry today during business hours.

**Step #2.** Go to irs.gov to register your Employer Identification Number (EIN) free, using form SS4. After the registration is complete, print the EIN document (Monday-Friday. Please check the website for registration guidelines as the rules change often)

**Step #3.** After you have printed the IRS SS4 Form, use your newly registered "EIN" at your selected bank to open a bank account in your business name only, you do not have to use your name and social security number; this will only be necessary if required by the bank you choose.

**REMEMBER THESE 5 REQUIREMENTS:**

1. Register your business name and file it with your State Business Registry or Secretary of State.
2. Obtain a Registered Agent (www.incfile.com). Note: only if necessary.
3. Obtain a Certificate of Formation from the office of your Secretary of State.
4. Prepare an Operating Agreement (forms can be found online).
5. Obtain an EIN from the IRS (irs.gov).

Once you have followed these exact legal steps to form your business, I will teach you step-by-step, "How to Access Thousands and Millions" in my informative step-by-step Masterclass. Once I show you how to do this, you can share this information with your family, you can do this for generations.

What would you do with $10K, $25K or $100K in 90 days? Follow these free legal steps and free tips I provided to get started. I have obtained these amounts in 180 days or less!!

Take these valuable and important tips and implement them into your life so you can get started taking the steps towards living your dreams.

*The conversion of cash to plastic is an unstoppable global trend.*
**Philip Philliou**

I have a goal to impact 2,500 people nationally and internationally, through my Masterclass- *How to Start a Business and Get Business Credit Now*.

Hey, I accessed over $1 million, and I did it in less than one year with the same resources you have. Would you be willing to invest a small amount in yourself for this master class if I agree to tell you exactly how I did it, so you can do it, too?

**Often, the masses are plundered and do not know it.**
**Frederic Bastiat**

*Dear Wealth Builders,*

*If you liked the information and free tips I have shared, then you would love my new Master Class Program which goes much deeper, providing step-by-step instructions on how you can access millions in funding and business credit quickly and in a short period of time. Building significant business credit and obtaining $200,000 to $2 million in business credit typically requires a structured and strategic approach.*

Which I show you how to do quickly.

## STEPS THAT YOU WILL EXPLORE IN THE MASTERCLASS:

1. **Incorporate Your Business-** Ensure that your business is legally registered as a separate entity, such as an LLC or Corporation. This establishes a clear separation between personal and business finances.
2. **Establish a Business Credit Profile-** Obtain an Employer Identification Number (EIN) from the IRS.
3. **Open a Business Bank Account-** Use it to handle your business finances separately.
4. **Apply for Business Credit Cards-** Start with business credit cards from issuers that report to business credit bureaus. Make on-time payments and keep credit utilization low to build a positive credit history.
5. **Trade Credit-** Establish relationships with suppliers and vendors who report payment history to business credit bureaus. Pay bills promptly to build credit.
6. **Apply for Secured Loans-** Consider applying for secured business loans or lines of credit, where you provide collateral to secure the credit.
7. **Participate in Business Credit Builder Programs-** Some companies offer programs specifically designed to help businesses build credit. These programs often involve making regular payments to a business savings account, which then helps establish creditworthiness.
8. **Monitor and Maintain-** Regularly monitor your business credit reports and scores. Correct any errors promptly. Maintain a good credit history by paying bills on time and managing your finances responsibly.
9. **Build a Strong Business Plan-** Lenders may require a solid business plan that demonstrates your business's viability and how you intend to use the credit.
10. **Network with Financial Institutions-** Establish relationships with banks and credit unions that offer business lending. Having a pre-existing relationship can be beneficial when seeking larger credit lines.
11. **Seek Professional Guidance-** Consult with financial advisors or credit-building experts who specialize in helping businesses obtain credit.

It's important to note that building substantial business credit in larger amounts takes time, often several years, so be patient and diligent in your efforts. However, I teach my students in the Masterclass, how to implement these strategies to obtain large amounts in a matter of 3-6 months. Additionally, lenders may have specific requirements and criteria for granting larger lines of credit, so be prepared to meet their standards and provide the necessary documentation.

**Here are all the additional benefits you'll obtain in your masterclass:**

- Informational Videos within Training Modules
- Example Documents from a Lender
- How to Complete Lender Forms
- Online Training Academy
- Upon Completion- a clear strategy to obtain tremendous amounts of business credit & funding!

I guarantee you no one can beat that value. *Especially with Results Like These!*

This Master Class with its complete training modules from A-Z, is designed to empower you to build and structure a business from beginning to end like an expert. Again, nothing is left to chance or guesswork here. If you have a question, the answer is here!

While individuals may spend time figuring things out on their own, it's more beneficial to seek a mentor. Here are a few key reasons why obtaining a mentor makes sense:

1. **Guidance and Expertise-** A mentor can provide valuable insight and expertise in various areas, and help you make informed decisions with vendors, finances, and other aspects of your business.
2. **Efficiency-** Instead of spending time researching and experimenting, a mentor can fast-track your learning, saving you precious time and resources.
3. **Networking-** Mentors often have a network of contacts and connections that can open doors to opportunities you might not discover on your own.
4. **Accountability-** A mentor can hold you accountable for your goals and help you stay on track, ensuring you make progress.
5. **Personal Growth-** Interactions with a mentor can foster personal growth, offering new perspectives and challenging you to improve.

In summary, having a mentor and participating in a Master Class can provide guidance, save time, expand your network, and contribute to your personal development; making it a wise choice in achieving business success and enhancing the quality of your life.

## ACTION STEPS:

Visit the website. Click on the video and register right now to get started!

For more free business credit tips and tools, visit and register today at:

Join By Phone: Text the word--------> KEYACCESS to "66866"

**Join the Tribe and Register:** www.thekeyaccess.com

Note: (Amazon Book Links and Business Credit Builder links provided by email upon your registration for the free tools or products)

**Join the Webinars and Purchase the Masterclass at:** www.SamanthaKUniversity.com. Launching a new website!!

**Amazon Book Link:**
http://amazon.com/dp/b01915qqi4/ref=cm_sw_r_sms_c_api_i_mwgtcbr3j3cyr_nodl/

**Like & Subscribe to YouTube Channel:**
@SamanthaKBond9580
https://youtube.com/@samanthakbond9580?si=4AmNPLlaLuzX47Kv

**Instagram:** @SamanthKBond

**Tik Tok:** TheKeyAccess @SamanthaKBond

Business Credit and Funding remains a hot and trending topic! Funding is a key concern for businesses, especially in challenging economic times and recessions.

I offer proven processes and established methods to assist businesses in establishing their business credit and securing funding.

These proven methods of tried-and-tested business credit and financing techniques deliver results!!"

**Get a FREE business credit consultation here:**
https://et128.isrefer.com/go/wwd/KeyAccessInt/

**After you complete the steps I've provided, get 12 lines of business credit here:** https://et128.isrefer.com/go/12clwbn/KeyAccessInt/

**JOIN VISIONARY AUTHOR AYANNA SMITH WEEKLY**

shero *publishing*

Made in the USA
Middletown, DE
29 January 2024

48727019R00060